Oxford Read and Discover

3

Free Time
Around the World

Julie Penn

Contents

OXFORD
UNIVERSITY PRESS

OXFORD
UNIVERSITY PRESS

Great Clarendon Street, Oxford OX2 6DP

Oxford University Press is a department of the University of Oxford. It furthers the University's objective of excellence in research, scholarship, and education by publishing worldwide in

Oxford New York

Auckland Cape Town Dar es Salaam Hong Kong Karachi Kuala Lumpur Madrid Melbourne Mexico City Nairobi New Delhi Shanghai Taipei Toronto

With offices in

Argentina Austria Brazil Chile Czech Republic France Greece Guatemala Hungary Italy Japan Poland Portugal Singapore South Korea Switzerland Thailand Turkey Ukraine Vietnam

OXFORD and OXFORD ENGLISH are registered trade marks of Oxford University Press in the UK and in certain other countries

No unauthorized photocopying

ISBN: 978 0 19 464378 8

An Audio Pack containing this book and an Audio download is also available, ISBN 978 0 19 402179 1

This book is also available as an e-Book, ISBN 978 0 19 410874 4.

An accompanying Activity Book is also available, ISBN 978 0 19 464388 7

Printed in China

This book is printed on paper from certified and well-managed sources.

ACKNOWLEDGEMENTS

Illustrations by: Kelly Kennedy pp.8, 11, 16, 21; Dusan Pavlic/ Beehive Illustration pp.24, 26, 30, 33, 34, 36, 38, 46-47; Alan Rowe pp.46-47.

The Publishers would also like to thank the following for their kind permission to reproduce photographs and other copyright material: Alamy pp.6 (dog sled/All Canada Photos), 8 (Ben Pipe), 12 (ton koene), 13 (Iain Masterson), 14 (WorldFoto), 15 (H. Mark Weidman Photography), 16 (Jorge Fernandez), 17 (boy and drum/Louise Batalla Duran, modern Nigerian music/Jeff Morgan 01), 18 (Gordon Scammell), 19 sandsurfer/Ingolf Pompe 25), 20 (Steppenwolf); Getty Images pp.3 (guitar/ Stockbyte), 4 (Christopher Pillitz/Hulton Archive), 5 (Evaristo Sa/AFP), 6 (snow mobile/Greg Ceo/Stone+), 11 (Jim Sugar/ The Image Bank Unreleased), 19 (beach cricket/Mark Nolan/ Stringer); Oxford University Press pp.3 (handlebars/skiing/ football/Photodisc/Getty, tent/Shutterstock), 9 (Photolibrary/ Getty), 21 (Cate Gillan/Getty), 22 (Shutterstock), 23 (Darryl Lenuik/Stockbyte/Getty), 28 (Photolibrary/Getty); Shutterstock pp.7 (Rob Crandall), 10 (Sipa/Shutterstock Editorial).

Introduction

Free time is very important. It's good for you to do something different after school or work. It's also fun! Many of our favorite free-time activities are popular all around the world.

Which activities can you see here?
What do you do in your free time?
What activities are popular in your country?

Discover!

Now read and discover more about free-time activities around the world!

3

1 Goal!

Playing Soccer, Brazil

Soccer is the most popular sport in the world and it's a big part of life in Brazil. People here love to watch and play soccer in their free time.

In Brazil you don't need a pitch or expensive boots to play soccer. People play soccer in the street and on the beach. Children often play with no boots.

Some people think that Brazilians are good at soccer because they learn a special way to play when they are children. They learn to play a type of soccer called futsal. There are five players in each team. The ball is small, but it's full of sand so it's very heavy.

Futsal started in South America, but now it's popular in many other countries.

Playing Futsal, Brazil

Go to pages 24–25 for activities.

2 Snow Sports

Dog Sledding

In Nunavut in the north of Canada, winter is from September to June. So there's a lot of time for snow sports. Skiing and tobogganing are very popular. Dog sledding is another exciting snow sport. The driver sits in the sled and the dogs pull it over the snow. Every year there is a big dog sled race.

Discover!

There aren't many roads in Nunavut. In winter most people travel by snowmobile or plane.

In Dubai in the United Arab Emirates, the summer is very hot. It's even warm in winter, but it's still a good place for snow sports!

Dubai has the biggest snow dome in the world. People come here for skiing, snowboarding, and tobogganing. It's very, very cold in the snow dome, but it's much hotter outside. The snow dome is in the desert!

In the Dubai Snow Dome, United Arab Emirates

Go to pages 26–27 for activities.

In India there are many different types of dance. Bollywood dance is very popular, and many people are learning it in their free time. This type of dance is fast and colorful.

Bollywood is the name of India's most famous movie industry. In Bollywood movies there is always singing and dancing.

Discover!

Bollywood is the biggest movie industry in the world. It makes about 1,000 movies every year.

Bollywood dancers wear colorful clothes. They also wear jewelry like earrings, necklaces, and lots of bangles. Between their eyebrows, they have a mark or jewel called a bindi.

Bollywood dance started in India, but now it's popular all around the world. You can watch a Bollywood movie or go to Bollywood dance lessons in lots of countries.

bangles

bindi

earring

necklace

➔ Go to pages 28–29 for activities.

4 Martial Arts

A Tae Kwon Do Class, South Korea

Tae kwon do is a national sport in South Korea and it's the most popular martial art in the world. About 70 million people in 188 different countries practice tae kwon do in their free time.

Tae kwon do means 'the way of hands and feet'. Students learn different moves with these parts of the body. They also learn how to balance, and how to control the body.

striped belt

white belt

Tae Kwon Do Students, USA

Students wear different-colored belts to show their level. The first belt is white. The other colors are yellow, green, blue, red, and black. When students are practicing for the next level, they wear a striped belt. The last belt is the black belt.

Discover!

In some schools in Korea there are Taeglish lessons. Students learn tae kwon do and English at the same time.

BACK KICK

Go to pages 30–31 for activities.

Let's Read!

All around the world, people like to read books, newspapers, magazines, and comic books. In Japan, reading manga is a really popular free-time activity.

Manga is a type of comic book. In manga there are words and pictures to tell a story or give information. There are lots of different types of manga, for example, adventure, mystery, science fiction, and comedy. There is manga for all ages.

In a Manga Bookshop, Japan

You can find manga on the Internet, too. There are also manga computer games and manga cartoons on television. There are even manga cafés, where you can look at manga on the Internet, or read manga books and magazines.

Manga started in Japan, but it's now popular in many countries. Some libraries in the USA have manga reading groups.

Go to pages 32–33 for activities.

6 At the Game

A Basketball Game, USA

Basketball is the most popular team sport in the USA. Many students are in school or college teams. Lots of other people play the game in their free time, on courts or in their gardens.

Basketball is a fast game. It's fun to play and it's fun to watch. People like to support their friends or family at the games. They also watch their favorite team on television.

Discover!

Basketball is very popular in China. About 300 million people play it, and 450 million people watch it on television.

Cheerleaders support their team at the games. About three million people in the USA are in cheerleading groups. Today most cheerleaders are female, but when cheerleading started it was only for men!

Cheerleading isn't easy. You have to be good at dance and gymnastics.

Cheerleaders at a Game

Go to pages 34–35 for activities.

7 Making Music

Traditional Nigerian Music

Music is very popular all around the world. It's a very important part of life in Nigeria, in Africa. People here sing, dance, and play music at important times in their lives.

In traditional Nigerian music, there is singing, and people play instruments. There are percussion instruments like drums, bells, and rattles. There are other instruments like pipes and trumpets, too.

Discover!

The kakaki trumpet can be 4 meters long. Only men play it.

Nigerian children sometimes make their own instruments. They make drums from tin cans, and pipes from plants. They also make rattles from fruits.

A Boy with a Drum

Lots of different types of modern music are popular in Nigeria, too. Some modern music, like jazz, reggae, and rock, came from traditional African music.

Modern Nigerian Music

Go to pages 36–37 for activities.

Beach Sports

In Australia there are about 26,000 kilometers of coast and about 11,000 beaches. Most people live near the ocean and many Australians spend a lot of their free time at the beach.

Many beaches in Australia are great for surfing. Kayaking, swimming, and snorkeling are popular water sports, too. Australia has thousands of surf lifeguards to keep the beaches safe.

Surfing

On the sand, people play beach volleyball and beach cricket. Beach cricket started as a fun activity, but now it's an official sport. There are beach cricket championships every year in Australia.

Discover! You can go sandsurfing on some beaches, and also in the desert in countries like Peru and Egypt.

➜ Go to pages 38–39 for activities.

9 Scouting

Scouting started in the United Kingdom in 1907. The first Scouts were boys from 11 to 18 years old. They went camping and walking in their free time. They learned how to read maps and make fires.

Today, Scouting isn't only for boys. Anyone from 6 to 25 years old can be a Scout. Scouts still go camping and walking, but there are lots of other exciting activities.

Scouts Learning to Sail

Scouts can do land activities like climbing and skateboarding, and water activities like sailing, kayaking, and snorkeling. Sometimes they can even do air activities like paragliding.

Scouts have fun, but they also work together to help other people and the countryside. Do you have Scouts in your country?

Discover! There are more than 28 million Scouts in 216 different countries.

Go to pages 40–41 for activities.

10 Let's Cycle!

Cycling, the Netherlands

Cycling is a very popular free-time activity all around the world. In the Netherlands about 85 percent (%) of people go cycling. Most of the land is flat, so it's a good place to cycle. It's also very safe. There are 17,000 kilometers of cycle paths, and most of the time, cars have to wait for bicycles.

BMX riding is another popular activity in many countries. There are two types of BMX riding – racing and freestyle.

BMX racers travel around a track and try to win a race. It isn't easy, and there are lots of jumps and turns. In BMX freestyle, riders do jumps and tricks. The best place to practice BMX freestyle is in a skatepark.

Which new free-time activities do you want to do now?

A BMX Rider in a Skatepark, Canada

→ Go to pages 42–43 for activities.

1 Goal!

← Read pages 4–5.

1 Write the words.

> boots ~~pitch~~ ball player team

1 __pitch__   2 _____   3 _____

4 _____   5 _____

2 Complete the sentences.

> sand ~~popular~~ street boots five

1 Soccer is the most __popular__ sport in the world.

2 In Brazil people play soccer in the _____.

3 Brazilian children often play soccer with no _____.

4 There are _____ players in each futsal team.

5 A futsal ball is full of _____.

3 Write *soccer* or *futsal*.

1 People play this game outside. <u>soccer</u>

2 There are five players in each team. _____

3 It's the most popular game in the world. _____

4 The ball is small. _____

5 The ball is heavy. _____

6 It started in South America. _____

4 Order the words.

1 popular / Soccer / very / a / sport. / is

<u>Soccer is a very popular sport.</u>

2 watching / playing / like / People / and / soccer.

_____

3 expensive / need / boots. / don't / You

_____

4 Brazilian / children / Many / futsal. / play

_____

5 five / There / a / team. / players / are / in / futsal

_____

6 ball / sand. / full / of / The / is / futsal

_____

② Snow Sports

← Read pages 6–7.

1 Find and write the snow sports.

1   __tobogganing__   3 _____

2 _____   4 _____

2 Write the words.

> cloudy   sunny   hot   warm   windy   cold

1 _____   2 _____   3 _____

4 _____   5 _____   6 _____

3 **Write *colder* or *hotter*.**

1 Winter in Nunavut is _____ than winter in Dubai.

2 The temperature in the snow dome is _____ than the temperature outside.

3 It's usually _____ in Dubai than in Nunavut.

4 Summer in Dubai is much _____ than summer in Nunavut.

4 **Answer the questions.**

1 What snow sports can you do in Nunavut?

   Skiing, tobogganing, and dog sledding.

2 What happens every year in Nunavut?

   _____

3 Can you go dog sledding in Dubai?

   _____

4 How is the weather outside the snow dome?

   _____

5 What sports do you do in summer?

   _____

6 What sports do you do in winter?

   _____

3 Let's Dance!

← Read pages 8–9.

1 Circle the correct words.

1 Bollywood dance started in (India) / **Japan**.

2 In Bollywood movies there is **sometimes** / **always** singing and dancing.

3 The dances are **slow** / **fast**.

4 The dancers wear **colorful** / **black** clothes.

5 Bollywood dance **is** / **isn't** popular in other countries.

6 Bollywood makes 1,000 **dances** / **movies** every year.

2 Write the words.

> necklace   earring
> bangles   bindi

1 _____

2 _____

3 _____

4 _____

3 Order the words.

1 dance. / many / of / there / different / In / India / are / types

_____

2 popular / world. / Bollywood / all / is / dance / around / the

_____

3 and / dance / fast / Bollywood / colorful. / is

_____

4 1,000 / makes / movies / about / year. / Bollywood / every

_____

5 wear / Bollywood / clothes / colorful / and / dancers / jewelry.

_____

4 Answer the questions.

1 Do you like dancing?

_____

2 What dances are popular in your country?

_____

3 What do people wear for these dances?

_____

4 Martial Arts

← Read pages 10–11.

1 Write *true* or *false*.

1 Tae kwon do is a national sport in the USA. _false_

2 It isn't popular in other countries. _____

3 It means 'the way of hands and feet'. _____

4 Students learn how to balance. _____

5 Students wear different-colored belts to show their age. _____

6 The first belt is the yellow belt. _____

2 Match.

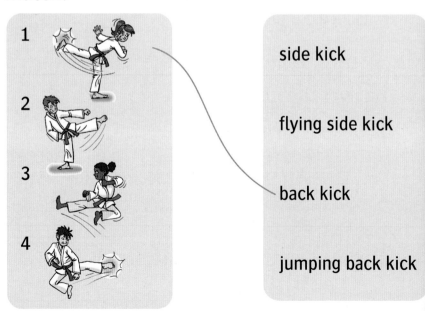

side kick

flying side kick

back kick

jumping back kick

3 Find and write the colors. Then color the belts.

1 white
2 y_____
3 g_____
4 b_____
5 r_____
6 b_____

c	g	b	r	h	i	n	a
e	r	l	o	r	e	d	k
t	e	a	s	y	e	t	b
y	e	l	l	o	w	o	l
o	n	e	n	s	h	g	u
a	k	g	i	j	i	l	e
b	l	a	c	k	t	c	p
f	u	m	r	v	e	u	e

4 Match. Then write the sentences.

About 70 million people

Students learn different moves

Students wear different-colored belts

The black belt is

In Taeglish lessons students learn

tae kwon do and English.

the last belt.

practice tae kwon do.

to show their level.

with their hands and feet.

1 About 70 million people practice tae kwon do.
2 _____
3 _____
4 _____
5 _____

31

⑤ Let's Read!

← Read pages 12–13.

1 **Find and write the things that you can read.**

r e b o o k r e n e w s p a p e r e r c o s t o r y

o k o n m a g a z i n e n i n c o m i c b o o k z

1 _____   4 _____

2 _____   5 _____

3 _____

2 **Write *true* or *false*.**

1 Manga started in Japan.   _____

2 Manga books don't have pictures.   _____

3 There's manga for all ages.   _____

4 There isn't any manga on the Internet.   _____

5 There are manga cafés in Japan.   _____

6 There are manga reading groups
   in the USA.   _____

3 Complete the puzzle.

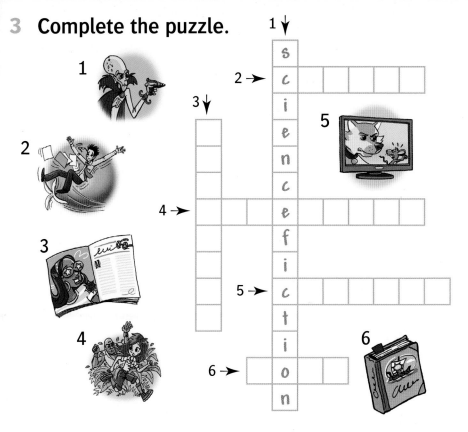

4 Answer the questions.

1 What do you read?

_____

2 When do you read?

_____

3 What is your favorite story?

_____

4 What do people like to read in your country?

_____

6 At the Game

← Read pages 14–15.

1 Write the words.

> cheerleaders   team   gymnastics   court

1 _____

3 _____

2 _____

4 _____

2 Circle the correct words.

1 Basketball is a **fast** / **slow** sport.

2 People play basketball in their **houses** / **gardens**.

3 Basketball **is** / **isn't** very popular in China.

4 Cheerleaders support their **teacher** / **team**.

5 There are **3** / **30** million cheerleaders in the USA.

6 Cheerleading **is** / **isn't** easy.

3 Write *basketball* or *cheerleading*.

1 It's the most popular team sport
  in the USA.   _____

2 Most people who do this activity
  are female.   _____

3 A lot of people play this game in
  their free time.   _____

4 You have to be good at dance
  to do this.   _____

5 You can watch your favorite
  team on television.   _____

4 Match. Then write the sentences.

Many students are in	dance and gymnastics.
You can play basketball	on television.
It's fun to watch basketball	college basketball teams.
Cheerleaders are good at	in a garden.

1 _____

2 _____

3 _____

4 _____

(7) Making Music

← Read pages 16–17.

1 Find and write the words.
Then complete the chart.

e	d	a	s	p	l	p
e	r	o	n	i	e	z
i	a	t	j	p	i	t
s	t	b	s	e	o	h
l	t	p	r	a	l	u
f	l	a	d	r	u	m
b	e	l	l	u	i	x
t	r	u	m	p	e	t

1 _____

2 _____   3 _____

4 _____   5 _____

Percussion Instruments	Other Instruments
_____	_____
_____	_____
_____	

2 **Complete the sentences.**

life   singing   plants   times   instruments

1 Music is an important part of _____ in Nigeria.

2 There is singing and dancing for important _____.

3 In traditional Nigerian music, there is _____ and people playing instruments.

4 Children sometimes make their own _____.

5 They make pipes from _____.

3 **Answer the questions.**

1 Do you like singing?

_____

2 Can you play any musical instruments?

_____

3 What is your favorite type of music?

_____

4 What type of music is popular in your country?

_____

_____

_____

8 Beach Sports

← Read pages 18–19.

1 Write the words. Then complete the chart.

swimming   surfing   volleyball
kayaking   cricket   snorkeling

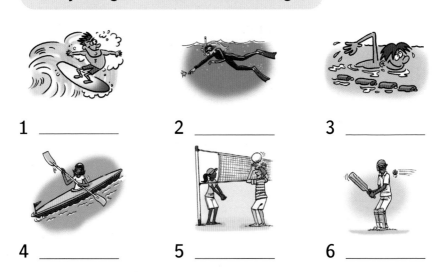

1 _____   2 _____   3 _____

4 _____   5 _____   6 _____

Water Sports	Sand Sports
_____	_____
_____	_____
_____	
_____	

2 Write *true* or *false*.

1 In Australia there are about 1,000 beaches. _____

2 Most people in Australia live near the ocean. _____

3 Many beaches in Australia are great for surfing. _____

4 People don't play cricket on the beach. _____

5 There are thousands of kayak lifeguards in Australia. _____

6 The lifeguards keep the beaches safe. _____

3 Answer the questions.

1 What beach sports can you do in Australia?

_____

2 Where can you go sandsurfing?

_____

3 What beach sports do you like?

_____

_____

_____

9 Scouting

← Read pages 20–21.

1 Find and write the activities. Then complete the diagram.

1 s _____
2 w _____
3 s _____
4 p _____
5 c _____
6 s _____
7 k _____
8 c _____

s	a	i	l	i	n	g	j	s
k	q	p	p	k	v	e	s	n
a	d	a	e	r	c	n	r	s
t	a	r	x	g	l	o	i	n
e	w	a	l	k	i	n	g	o
b	c	g	p	c	m	s	k	r
o	x	l	y	a	b	e	a	k
a	h	i	o	d	i	h	y	e
r	u	d	e	p	n	n	a	l
d	d	i	w	i	g	f	k	i
i	f	n	l	g	i	n	i	n
n	c	g	l	a	s	u	n	g
g	c	a	m	p	i	n	g	g

Air Activities

_____

Land Activities

_____

_____

_____

Water Activities

_____ _____

_____

40

2 Write the numbers.

25   1907   216   28   11   6   18

1 Scouting started in _____ .

2 When Scouting started it was for boys from
_____ to _____ years old.

3 Today, anyone from _____ to _____ years
old can be a Scout.

4 More than _____ million people around the
world are Scouts.

5 There are Scouts in _____ different countries.

3 Answer the questions.

1 When did Scouting start?

_____

2 Who were the first Scouts?

_____

3 What did the first Scouts learn to do?

_____

4 Who can be a Scout today?

_____

5 Which Scouting activities do you want to try?

_____

_____

10 Let's Cycle!

← Read pages 22–23.

1 Circle the correct words.

1 **Climbing** / **Cycling** is very popular in the Netherlands.

2 The land is flat, so it's a **good** / **bad** place to cycle.

3 There are 17,000 kilometers of cycle **parts** / **paths**.

4 In the Netherlands **25**% / **85**% of people go cycling.

5 Cars have to wait for **bicycles** / **planes**.

2 Write *cycling* or *BMX*.

1 There are special paths for this. _____

2 You can do this on a track or in a skatepark. _____

3 There are two types – freestyle and racing. _____

4 It's a good sport for where the land is flat. _____

3 **Match. Then write the sentences.**

BMX riding is popular	is in a skatepark.
There are two types	of BMX riding.
You can do BMX racing	in many countries.
The best place to practice BMX freestyle	around a track.

1 _____

2 _____

3 _____

4 _____

4 **Answer the questions.**

1 What type of cycling is popular in your country?

_____

2 Which do you like best, cycling or BMX riding?

_____

3 Which new free-time activities do you want to do?

_____

_____

_____

My Free-Time Diary

1 Keep a record of the free-time activities that you do in a week. Write them in this diary.

Monday	Friday
Tuesday	Saturday
Wednesday	
	Sunday
Thursday	

2 At the end of the week write about the activities.

On Monday I went to reading club. We read a book by Roald Dahl. It was very funny. We all liked it.

On Tuesday I played soccer with my friends ...

A Free-Time Survey

1 Write four more free-time activities in the chart.

2 Interview your friends and family. Write ✔ or ✗.

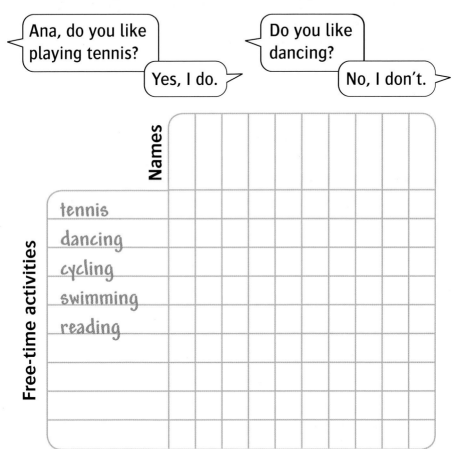

Ana, do you like playing tennis?

Yes, I do.

Do you like dancing?

No, I don't.

Names

Free-time activities

tennis
dancing
cycling
swimming
reading

3 Count how many people like each activity. What's the most popular free-time activity?

4 Display your results.

Picture Dictionary

 adventure

 balance

 bell

 camping

 cartoon

 climbing

 clothes

 coast

 comedy

 countryside

 court

 cycle path

 desert

 drum

 female

 fire

 flat

 jewel

 kayaking

 land

lifeguard
 magazine
 male
 million
 mystery

 newspaper
 ocean
 paragliding
 percent (%)
 pipe

 pitch
 plants
 rattle
 sailing
 sand

 science fiction
 snorkeling
 street
 team

tobogganing

Oxford Read and Discover

Series Editor: Hazel Geatches • CLIL Adviser: John Clegg

Oxford Read and Discover graded readers are at six levels, for students from age 6 and older. They cover many topics within three subject areas, and support English across the curriculum, or Content and Language Integrated Learning (CLIL).

Available for each reader:
- Audio Pack
- Activity Book

Available for selected readers:
- e-Books

Teaching notes & CLIL guidance: **www.oup.com/elt/teacher/readanddiscover**

Subject Area / Level	The World of Science & Technology	The Natural World	The World of Arts & Social Studies
1 — 300 headwords	• Eyes • Fruit • Trees • Wheels	• At the Beach • In the Sky • Wild Cats • Young Animals	• Art • Schools
2 — 450 headwords	• Electricity • Plastic • Sunny and Rainy • Your Body	• Camouflage • Earth • Farms • In the Mountains	• Cities • Jobs
3 — 600 headwords	• How We Make Products • Sound and Music • Super Structures • Your Five Senses	• Amazing Minibeasts • Animals in the Air • Life in Rainforests • Wonderful Water	• Festivals Around the World • Free Time Around the World
4 — 750 headwords	• All About Plants • How to Stay Healthy • Machines Then and Now • Why We Recycle	• All About Desert Life • All About Ocean Life • Animals at Night • Incredible Earth	• Animals in Art • Wonders of the Past
5 — 900 headwords	• Materials to Products • Medicine Then and Now • Transportation Then and Now • Wild Weather	• All About Islands • Animal Life Cycles • Exploring Our World • Great Migrations	• Homes Around the World • Our World in Art
6 — 1,050 headwords	• Cells and Microbes • Clothes Then and Now • Incredible Energy • Your Amazing Body	• All About Space • Caring for Our Planet • Earth Then and Now • Wonderful Ecosystems	• Food Around the World • Helping Around the World